ELIZABETHAN ENGLAND

BY ANTHONY WEST

ILLUSTRATED BY PETER SPIER

THE ODYSSEY PRESS · NEW YORK

ELIZABETH'S ENGLAND was a small country with no more than four and a half million people, and it was easy for the Queen to keep up an almost personal relationship with her subjects. She was, in fact, forced to do so because, although she had the final voice in all decisions on matters of state, she had no standing army and no paid bureaucracy to enforce and carry out her commands. She was as dependent on the good will of the majority as a politician is in a modern democracy. This was why she allowed her courtiers to foster the cult of her personality as Oriana, the solitary virgin goddess-queen who belonged to no man and was mistress to all her people.

Elizabethan Englishmen were sure that London was the "finest city of the world," but its narrow, twisting streets and alleyways lined with timber-framed houses, its filth, its smells, its noise and uproar, its plagues, and its crimes appalled foreigners. Elizabethan towns were small. The largest, London, held a quarter of a million people; few others had as many as ten thousand inhabitants. The countryside was never further off than the end of the next street.

She collaborated to the full in the making of her own legend, but, although she appeared to have an unlimited appetite for flattery, she was no fool, and always took good care to see that her policies were in line with her people's wishes. ■ She governed through her council of ministers, and through the remains of the old medieval bureaucracy. This had once been operated by clerks in holy orders, but it had been converted by the earlier Tudors into a patronage machine. The Elizabethan who entered the government service drew a small salary, but his real income came from the fees that he was entitled to charge for carrying out

Henry the Eighth, Elizabeth's father, lifted the hand of the Church from almost a third of the real property in the country when he broke with Rome and made England Protestant. The release of this locked-up capital brought English trade and commerce to life and laid the foundations of Elizabethan prosperity.

With Elizabeth's coronation procession, England began its march out of the medieval and into the modern world. The first English printing press had been set up at Westminster just over sixty years before she came to the throne, and fifty years after her death Parliament was faced with the first popular movement demanding the vote for every adult. As the Queen-to-be rode from the Tower of London to Westminster Abbey with a relatively small escort of guards and noblemen, she passed emblematic displays of brightly painted figures erected along the route by the merchants and tradesmen of London. Almost all had a common theme. In the language of symbol and allegory, they urged her to break her predecessor Mary's alliances with Spain and Rome, binding England to its medieval past, and to give her people a fresh start. When the crown was placed on her head she knew that her people were eager for its future.

9

his duties. ■ The secret of the success of Elizabeth's great minister William Cecil, Lord Burghley, was largely the mastery of the art of distributing patronage in such a way as to bind the powerful and influential families to the crown by the bond of common interest. Burghley's private papers show that he numbered the peers and gentlemen of real political importance in the country at just about a hundred, and the wealthy landowners at eight hundred. Burghley's lists also show that he considered some forty Lords and gentlemen fit for commands at sea, and nearly sixty qualified for employment as generals. He had between two and three thousand offices of profit to dispose of, and there were about five thousand members of

Elizabeth's foreign policy is to a large extent explained by this map and the Earl of Sussex's remark that "the case will be hard with the Queen and with England if ever the French possess or the Spaniards tyrannize in the Low Countries." It can be seen how if Spain or France controlled the Low Countries, England would be shut out of Germany, then her principal overseas market. It can also be seen why ardently Roman Catholic Spain was anxious to secure the Low Countries in order to thrust a wedge between Protestant England and Protestant Germany. England was bound to resist this effort to split Protestant Europe.

An Elizabethan description of the Tower of London says: "This tower is a citadel, to defend or command the city; a Royal place for assemblies and treaties. A Prison of Estate, for the most dangerous prisoners: the only place of coinage for all England at this time: the armory of warlike provision; the Treasury of the ornaments and jewels of the crown, and general conserver of the most records of the High Courts of Justice at Westminster." There was also a small zoo inside the walls, where lions were to be seen. One of the vessels lying off the Tower wharf in the illustration might be the Queen's ship Tyger, drawing £400 worth of gunpowder from the royal stores before sailing with Sir Richard Grenville's expedition to plant the first English colony in the new world in Virginia.

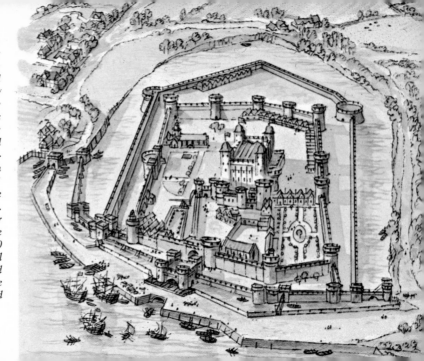

the ruling class in competition for them. Some of those who did not get places were given export or import licenses, trading monopolies, or grants allowing them to collect rents from tenants of crown lands. These favors, and all appointments in the government service, had to be sought at court, where the applicant might be kept hanging about to live on hope deferred for months or even years. ■ There were roughly a thousand people at Elizabeth's court. Most of them were household servants, guards, hunts-

Elizabeth's Parliaments were elected by landowners, town property owners, and prosperous merchants. The members they chose generally approved the Queen's policies and the Crown and the Parliament were rarely in conflict during her reign. Its principal achievement was the Statute of Artificers, a bill regulating conditions of labor and workshop practices which remained in force until the beginning of the 19th century.

An insatiable appetite for futile intrigues made the Roman Catholic princess Mary Queen of Scots a problem that her Protestant kinswoman Elizabeth was finally forced to solve with the headsman's axe.

men, grooms, and workmen, but two hundred were the peers, ladies, and gentlemen in attendance, and the household officers making up the Queen's personal entourage. ■ The Queen has been called vain because she had two thousand dresses when she died, and because she always wore costly materials and splendid jewels, even when she was on the hunting field. It wasn't, however, simple vanity that led her to adorn herself. She was in an unprecedented position as a crowned head and an unmarried woman, and it was imperative that she should always be visibly the sovereign and never the ordinary mortal. ■ She had many reasons to feel insecure. Her mother, Anne Boleyn, the second

By Elizabeth's time, the old palace of Westminster, lying between the Abbey and the Thames, had become the home of Parliament, the law courts and the royal bureaucracy. It was at Whitehall, a new palace beyond the Abbey, that the Queen received Tsar Boris Godunov's ambassador in 1601.

wife of Henry VIII, was beheaded when Elizabeth was not quite three, and her third, and favorite, stepmother, was killed in the same way when she was in her tenth year. Two years after the death of her father in 1547, when she was sixteen, her first love, Thomas Seymour, was executed for treason, having tried to make use of her in a plot to remove her consumptive half-brother Edward VI from the throne. When Edward soon after died, and was succeeded by Elizabeth's elder half-sister Mary, her situation became hideous. Mary was the Roman Catholic child of Henry's first wife, the Spanish princess Catherine of Aragon. As soon as she was Queen she married the ultra-Catholic Philip of Spain and set to work to destroy the national Church, Protestant in theology and independent of Rome, which had been established by Henry. Many Englishmen were bitterly opposed to this and wished to bring Elizabeth, who was known as the Protestant Princess, to the throne in her place. As a result, Elizabeth lived through Mary's reign, from her twentieth to her twenty-fifth year, under suspicion, and at times under arrest. A few careless words, or an ambiguous sentence in a letter, that could be twisted to show knowledge of some plot, could at any time bring her neck under the axe. ■ As soon as she became Queen, she learned in the most brutal fashion how vulnerable she was. She was crowned in January, 1559. By April it was being said all over Europe that she was in love with Lord Robert Dudley, and that they would

John Whitgift, Archbishop of Canterbury, was the Queen's able champion in the long battle between the Crown and the Puritan divines for control of the Anglican Church. The chief of his opponents was John Field, who wished to carry the reform of the church much further in the direction of Presbyterianism.

be married as soon as his wife was dead of the cancer of the breast from which she was suffering. This ugly rumor was given an even uglier turn by the death of Dudley's wife. She was found with her neck broken at the foot of a staircase in her country house. It was said that she had been murdered to clear the way for her husband's marriage to the Queen. The resulting scandal may well have been decisive in convincing Elizabeth that she could not live the life of an ordinary woman and keep her crown. She certainly never considered marriage with a subject thereafter. ■ Elizabeth had still other reasons for feeling unsure of her position. Roman Catholics contended that the marriage between her mother and father was invalid and

Sir William Cecil, Lord Burghley, Elizabeth's first secretary of state, grew old and rich in her service. When worn out by too much work and too much company, he found relief in riding privately in his gardens on his little mule.

that Elizabeth could not therefore be the lawful heir to the throne. In their view, the successor to Mary should have been Henry VII's great-granddaughter, Mary Stuart, Queen of Scots and wife to the king of France. ∎ France was then in rivalry with Spain for mastery of the Low Countries and for domination in Western Europe; it was obvious that France had a great deal to gain by setting up an Anglo-French kingdom straddling the Channel and Spain's shortest route to Holland and Flanders. It therefore became an aim of French policy to persuade the Pope to proclaim Elizabeth's illegitimacy as a prelude to organizing a Roman Catholic Rebellion in England which would put Mary on the throne. This policy made France the most immediate threat to England in the opening years of Elizabeth's reign and led her to seek safety in alliance with Spain. ∎ The French threat, however, disappeared when internal dis-

Hardwick Hall, with its symmetrical plan and its precisely balanced composition of masses, is one of the earliest English houses to show a real understanding of the Renaissance style. Robert Smythson, who designed it and also Longleath House, was one of the first Englishmen who can be called a professional architect (as opposed to a master-mason, in the medieval tradition).

17

Sir Francis Drake (LEFT) went to sea at the age of eleven, apprenticed to the master of a cargo vessel in the North Sea trade, and rose to be the Queen's favorite captain. Sir John Hawkins (RIGHT) was the shrewd administrator who gave the Queen fast ships and good guns. (BELOW) The Ark Royal was the flagship from which the Lord Admiral directed the fight against the Spanish Armada in 1588. She was a hundred feet in length with a beam of thirty-seven feet, and displaced just under seven hundred tons. Room was found on her three decks for a company of four hundred men, thirty-two of them gunners.

sensions, which culminated in the massacre of the Huguenots on St. Bartholomew's Eve, drove Mary Queen of Scots out of the country and caused a collapse of France as a military power. Elizabeth now had to reverse her alliances and to support France against Spain to check an excessive growth of Spanish power in Northern Europe. Spain then sought a declaration of Elizabeth's illegitimacy and a rebellion of her Catholic subjects. ■ The first object was attained

Drake's willingness to take the tiny Golden Hind into action against the huge Spanish treasure ships (RIGHT) stemmed from the knowledge that he was using a well designed warship (ABOVE) to attack cumbersome, lightly armed merchantmen.

There were two "families" of Elizabethan seamen in the Atlantic. One derived from the Bristol merchants who followed the Portuguese pioneers into the Newfoundland fishery, and became interested in the Northwest passage. The other stemmed from the Cornish and Breton pirates who preyed on Spanish trading vessels returning from the Americas and became interested in planting American colonies.

19

The great Armada, sailing in half moon formation, passed up the Channel without serious interference from the English fleet. Its mission was to support an invasion of southern England by the Spanish troops in Flanders, who were supposed to have secured a base for it in the Scheldt estuary. When it arrived, however, the lower Scheldt was still controlled by the Dutch, and its commander found that he was expected to operate from the open roadsteads off Dunkirk and Gravelines. While the Armada was at anchor off the latter place, the English had their first success against it in a night attack. This unnerved the Spanish commander, who then made the catastrophic  decision to abandon his mission and go home. A second successful English attack on the following day convinced him that he could not beat down the Channel, against the prevailing wind, in the face of opposition. He accordingly decided to sail home round northern Scotland and Ireland. On this long cruise through unfamiliar waters, bad weather, disease, and starvation wrought havoc with the Armada. Of the one hundred twenty Spanish ships that had reached Gravelines, sixty-three were wrecked. Losses on board those ships that succeeded in reaching their home ports amounted to as much as half the company in many cases, and large numbers of the survivors died of exhaustion after their return. Of the eighteen thousand soldiers who left Spain in the Armada, only five thousand returned.

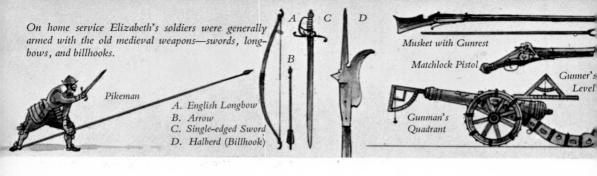

On home service Elizabeth's soldiers were generally armed with the old medieval weapons—swords, longbows, and billhooks.

Pikeman

A. English Longbow
B. Arrow
C. Single-edged Sword
D. Halberd (Billhook)

Musket with Gunrest

Matchlock Pistol

Gunner's Level

Gunman's Quadrant

in 1570, by which time the situation had been complicated by Mary Stuart's expulsion from Scotland as the consequence of her squalid involvements with Darnley and Bothwell. A born intriguer with a marked absence of common sense, she could not resist the temptation of plotting against Elizabeth even when she was a refugee on English soil. She had a finger in pitiful conspiracies against Elizabeth's life in 1583, 1585, and 1586, and then, having outworn the patience of the Queen and the Parliament, paid the penalty for her futile treasons in 1587. She had played one last bizarre trick on the English by naming Philip of Spain as the heir to her claim to the English throne, on the ground that he had a better right to the crown than Elizabeth, as a descendant of John of Gaunt in the female line. ■ In spite of Spain's

Drafts for foreign duty were issued pikes, muskets, and calivers, such as were used by European armies. Pikes were from 10 to 18 feet long. Ranging devices were sound in theory but of little real use because each batch of gunpowder varied in strength.

Guns became serious military weapons when the unreliable medieval breechloaders gave way to muzzleloaders that could stand heavy charges. The guns would be firing twenty to thirty pound shot. The wickerwork fascines round the guns were filled with earth or sand to protect the gunners from enemy fire. In the first phase of Elizabeth's Spanish war, it was all-important for the English to prevent the enemy from gaining possession of a North Sea base. There was consequently much bitter fighting between the Duke of Parma's Spaniards and the Anglo-Dutch garrisons in the walled towns controlling the shelters and havens along the coast. The defeat of the Armada was in large part due to the success of the English ground forces which had denied it a place of refuge by holding on to Bergen, Ostend, Flushing and Brielle, and keeping control of the mouth of the Scheldt. Later in the war there was more hard fighting between English and Spanish troops in Brittany, for possession of the harbor at Brest, and further north for the French channel ports. Unlike the Spanish, the English used no soldiers on their ships; they were manned by sailors.

23

A part of Queens' College, Cambridge, shows the type of heavy timber-framed construction characteristic of the early years of Queen Elizabeth's reign.

aim of putting her off her throne, Elizabeth's goal was limited to securing a balance of power on the shores of the Atlantic and the North Sea. She had no intention of destroying the power of Spain. Sir Walter Raleigh spoke for most of Elizabeth's fighting men when he expressed his dislike for this strategy soon after James I had come to the throne and ended nineteen years of war. "If the late Queen would have believed her men of war as she did her scribes we had in her time beaten that great empire in pieces and made their kings kings of figs and oranges as they were in old times. But her majesty did all by halves...." Raleigh's imagination, and that of his generation, had been caught by the dream of taking all the wealth of South America and the Indies from Spain. He could not understand the calculations of statecraft in which the independence of the Dutch Republic and the recovery of France were the great prizes of the war. The exploits of Elizabeth's sailors on the Spanish main were, in fact, far less important to her than futile campaigns in the Low Countries and France. Her soldiers fought in companies of a hundred men led by captains

Elizabethan Oxford was still a medieval school of theology set down in a small market town.

and officered by a lieutenant, an ensign, and two sergeants. Each company would normally muster a drummer, a flute-player, a barber-surgeon, thirty pikemen, thirty musketeers and forty men armed with a lighter firearm, roughly equivalent to a carbine, called a caliver. ■ Companies were raised when an expedition was planned. The Queen's commission calling for so many men from each county was sent to the Lords Lieutenant, who made up their drafts both by calling for volunteers and by clearing the jails of able-bodied men and the country-side of rogues and vagabonds. The men were armed and clothed to strict government specifi-

25

London Bridge carried the great road from Canterbury and Dover into London. The gate at its southern end was usually ornamented in Elizabethan times with the pickled heads of a dozen or more traitors. Its twenty-one piers, the corn mills blocking some of the arches, and the waterworks built at the southern end in 1582, made it function as a weir, so that shooting the bridge on an ebbing tide was exciting and dangerous. Most of the three thousand watermen who plied for hire on the river in those days liked to show their skill at the bridge, but most of their passengers liked to be put ashore at the old Swansteps above the bridge (AT LOWER LEFT) in order to walk on Billingsgate wharf below it.

cations, and then marched off to the port of embarkation, where the expedition's Muster Master assigned them to companies. Companies were brigaded by fives, to form regiments during campaigns, but there was no regimental organization. ■ Men died like flies when campaigning. The fate of the contingent of 4,000 men sent into France one September, which had lost three quarters of its strength by December, was typical. What survived of a company was broken up and the men were paid off as soon as the expeditionary force returned home. The only troops kept in the country were the groups of twelve to fifteen men on garrison duty in the thirty-five coastal ports, and two or three companies forming the garrison of Berwick near the Scottish border. Because ships needed repair and upkeep, the Elizabethan navy had the

The English landscape was changing fast in Elizabeth's day as community farming gave way to individual enterprise.

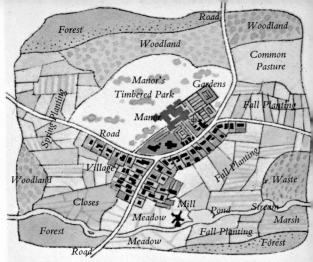

In the village above, one of the old open fields has been turned into the deer park of the manor house, and the others have been broken up into small enclosures surrounded by fences or hedges. In effect a big cooperative has been broken up into farms and small holdings. Isolated farm houses were also becoming a feature of the English scene.

The Queen's progresses through the countryside were pageants of loyalty. When she went into Suffolk in 1578, the sheriff rode out to meet her, accompanied by two hundred young men in white velvet, three hundred older men in black, and fifteen hundred serving men. All were mounted, and the two thousand horsemen escorted her from the county line to her destination. The object was to show the Queen to the people and to show the people's attachment to the crown. Her carriages were consequently more for parade than for practical use, and she rarely rode in them except when making a formal approach to a town or great house where she was expected. She is seen (ABOVE) riding in state on the road to Windsor Castle, while three of her coaches, a baggage cart and a carrier's wagon are seen below.

beginnings of a permanent structure inherited from Henry VII. Five Royal dockyards at Chatham, Woolwich, Deptford, Plymouth, and Portsmouth saw to the needs of the Queen's thirty ships, and questions of policy and supply were the concern of the Navy Board, a sub-committee of the Privy Council, presided over by a permanent official with the title of Lord High Admiral. ■ Luckily for Elizabeth, a successful slave trader and privateer, Sir John Hawkins, joined this board in the early 1570's, and won Lord Burghley and the board over to a new conception of fighting at sea. The older generation of sailors

The service in Elizabethan inns was lavish and good, but fleas and smelly privies and stables caused frequent complaints.

Elizabethan London had a multitude of taverns and ale houses with such names as the Kings Head, the Crown, the Golden Fleece, the Plough, the Star, the Rose, the Feathers, the Globe, the Drum, the White Hart, the Swan, the Worlds End, and so on. The most famous were the Mitre and the Mermaid, the first known in its time for its good food and drink, the second known forever because of its company, which included Shakespeare, Ben Jonson, Beaumont, Fletcher, Donne, and Sir Walter Raleigh. Other well known literary taverns were the Devil at Temple Bar, home of Raleigh's Apollo Club, and the Pegasus in Cheapside. The drinks sold were mostly wines and beers; spirits and hard liquor had not yet come into common use.

Although made of wood, Elizabethan machinery was surprisingly sophisticated. Windmills did a lot of work in dry districts, but watermills were common. Much water power was used in mining (BELOW) and the textile industry.

believed in winning a decision by boarding enemy vessels after clearing their decks with fire effective at short range. English iron masters had lately learned how to make long-range guns, and Sir John believed that by using these new guns on fast ships, he could win in gunfights without boarding. It would no longer be necessary to crowd warships with a mass of soldiery; ships could be kept at sea for longer periods without revictualing and with less risk of suffering heavy losses from disease. ■ Lord Burghley backed Sir John's plans for new ship design, and saw to it that the fleet would have the best powder for the new guns by cornering the whole of Morocco's output of saltpeter. He also ordered all trained gunners in England to register for national service in 1586, and made it unlawful for men on the register to leave England. As a result, the English fleet had a small but vital technical lead when it met the

Spanish Armada in 1588. Morale, too, was better on the English ships. The soldiers aboard the Spanish ships looked on their sailors as their menials, while the English ships were captained, worked, and fought by seamen. ■ Much as England owed to Sir John Hawkins, it may have owed still more to Sir Francis Walsingham. He urged the Queen to support the privateers and adventurers who wished to carry the war with Spain into the world's far corners. The consequences of his advocacy are perfectly summed up by Hakluyt, the contemporary chronicler of England's entry into world trade: "For which of the kings of this land before Her Majesty had their banners ever seen in the Caspian Sea? Which of them hath ever dealt with the Emperor of Persia...who ever found English consuls and agents at Tripolis in Syria, at Aleppo, at Babylon, at Balsara, and which is more who ever heard of Englishmen at Goa before now?

In Elizabethan London shops were generally attached to the workrooms in which the goods they sold were produced, and the shopkeeper was as a rule a tradesman or craftsman. He lived over his shop, and his apprentices and employees boarded with him. Tradesmen tended to cluster together in quarters and streets, so that the annalist Stow could record the changes that had taken place since medieval times: "For whereas Mercers and Haberdashers used to keep their shoppes in West Cheape, of later time they held them on London Bridge . . . the Goldsmiths of Gutherns Lane and old Exchange are now for the most part removed into the Southside of West Cheape," and so on.

BELOW, *some favorite Elizabethan instruments, and* TOP RIGHT, *a typical orchestra of the happiest period in English musical history.* BOTTOM RIGHT, *a glimpse of Will Kemp in action. He was the enormously popular comedian at the Globe Theatre, who once danced from London to Norwich to the music of pipe and tabor. His mugging and ad-libbing exasperated Shakespeare, who put some sharp words on the subject into Hamlet's mouth.*

What English ships did heretofore ever anchor in the mighty river Plate, pass and repass the impassable in former opinion strait of Magellan, range along the coast of Chile, Peru and all the backside of Nova Hispania...and last of all return home most richly laden with the commodities of China, as the subjects of this now flourishing monarchy have done?" ■ This Richard Hakluyt wrote the *Discourse of Western Planting* that Sir Walter Raleigh gave to the Queen when he was trying to win her support for his proposal to set up an English colony in North America. Convinced, she contributed money and the ship *Tyger* to the venture, which led to the first settlements in Virginia, in 1585-86. Raleigh's friend, Thomas Hariot, acquired the habit of smoking tobacco when he was in the new colony, became a heavy smoker, and lived into the reign of James I to die of cancer of the mouth. ■ Another man whose talk and writing interested the Queen in North America was John Dee, the Welsh astrologer and mapmaker, at whose door

This young man caught in the briars of love may be the Earl of Essex. The portrait is by Nicholas Hilliard, goldsmith and miniaturist, who was one of the court painters and a protege of Lord Burghley.

in Mortlake her coach often stopped. Her coachman, Willem Boonen, a Dutchman, brought the first coach into England in 1564, and Elizabeth was the first monarch to own a gold state carriage. Her traveling coach was of red leather studded with gilt nails. ■ In spite of her example, coaches did not come into common use in her time. Wealthy travelers used them in and around London, where they could be hired, but most people rode or walked when they had a journey to make. Horses could be hired by the day, week or month from inns, which also served as stations for the covered wagons run by carriers who took passengers and baggage from town to town. Goods and merchandise either went by water, on barges or flatboats on inland waterways, and in hoys and cobles between coastal ports, or they were moved by cart or pack-horse train. Drake's treasure was moved by pack-horse train from Deptford to London after the

Golden Hind's voyage round the world—another speculative venture in which the Queen was a shareholder. ■ When the Queen's court moved, she rode in her coach, and was followed by three hundred carts of baggage and her thousand courtiers and attendants riding on horseback. She was fond of traveling by water and often used her state barges to take her from one to another of her riverside palaces—Greenwich, Whitehall, Richmond, and Hampton Court. ■ Elizabeth seems to have been a restless Queen even by modern standards of reasonable mobility, but considerations of health, and her strong dislike of the smell of over-burdened stables and privies were her motives for moving her court as often as she did. Her godson Sir John Harrington gave this matter thought, and invented the first water closet to be put into use

Queen Elizabeth dancing with the Earl of Leicester.

Most Elizabethans sat at trestle tables on stools or benches when they ate, and slept on truckle beds that could be put out of the way in the daytime. Such heavy, coarsely carved, and ugly pieces, as those above, were reserved for the very rich. The bedding of the four-poster would have been carried on a criss-cross of ropes; complete with curtains and feather mattress, it cost as much as a Cadillac does today.

in England. One of his devices was installed in Richmond Palace, close to the looking-glass-lined bathing room that was a part of the Queen's suite. ■ Elizabeth inherited so many recently built palaces that she had no need to build. Her subjects, however, were astonishingly active in this respect. The price of glass, which fell to a reasonable level for the first time in the early part of her reign, had an effect on the Elizabethan style summed up in the descriptive couplet, "Hardwick Hall/More glass than wall." The small openings characteristic of earlier architectural styles gave way to large windows, which were, with increased frequency, symmetrically placed in symmetrical facades. ■ Fireplaces ousted the old hearths, as flues and chimneys came in with cheaper brick, and the falling price of white plaster changed the character of walls and ceilings. Upholstered furniture became common in rich houses and everywhere backed chairs took the place of stools and benches. The great advances in domestic comfort that took place in Elizabeth's time were once thought to be connected with the emergence of a new middle class, but recent research shows that what occurred was the enrichment of the gentry and the already existing urban middle class by a great boom in trade and manufacturing. The first textile factory, in which there were over a hundred looms, and in which over three hundred people were employed in turning raw wool into finished cloth, was established at Newbury in this period, and with the help of German technical advice a start was made in the serious exploita-

The great "prodigy" houses of the new Elizabethan nobility were surrounded by elaborate formal gardens and plantings imitated from French and Flemish designs. Many new and improved vegetables and flowers were brought into English gardens during the reign.

tion of England's mineral resources. ■ This boom was set off by Henry VIII's dissolution of the monasteries after 1535 and the subsequent redistribution of approximately a third of the real property in the country among the Protestant supporters of the monarchy. Elizabeth's succession made certain that this dispensation was final; it caused the confident surge of economic activity that stimulated and supported the cultural flowering which gave her reign its glory. ■ The substitution of English for Latin in the offices of the church gave Englishmen a fresh confidence in the use of their own tongue. Still an obscure island dialect when Elizabeth came to the throne, it became, before she died, the rich and subtle language of which such men as Shakespeare, Marlowe, Ben Jonson, Edmund Spenser, and Sir Philip Sidney were the makers and the masters. ■ The reform in the church also produced an abundance of lovely

Elizabethans took Monday as a day for play. The law required them to practice archery, but as firearms came in, interest in the bow went out. The men shooting at a target on a range (ABOVE) with crossbows were following a dying sport. Popular among the rich, who could afford the special indoor court, was the French game of tennis (RIGHT). A form of lawn tennis played outdoors with five men to a side was demonstrated to the Queen, but it failed to catch on. Hunting was the universal recreation. A page from a book published in 1575 (OPPOSITE PAGE) shows Queen Elizabeth at a hunt breakfast with staghounds. Foxes were then not hunted by gentlemen.

Footballers inflating a football, which was kept softer than the present practice. The game was quickly growing in popularity.

music to meet the needs of the new liturgy, and the work of its composers—Christopher Tye, Orlando Gibbons, William Byrd, Robert Parsons, William Damon and Thomas Tallis—if not great, consistently reaches the level of delight. ■ Elizabeth herself greatly enjoyed listening to music and playing the virginals and the lute. These were the instruments that all educated men and women then learned to play, just as they learned to sing. It was consequently a happy time for lyric verses, songs, and madrigals, and for the sort of light music in which Thomas Morley and John Dowland excelled. ■ The Queen took special pleasure in such singing, and, when she had turned seventy, her generosity to singers and musicians won her the tribute of a set of madrigals specially written in her honor by twenty-three composers. The Queen loved to dance, too, and there is a pleasant account of her being seen in her private apartments at Hampton Court when she was last there, in 1599, in the fortieth year of her reign, "dancing the Spanish panic to a whistle and tabor, none being with her but my Lady Warwick." ■ Elizabeth is and will always remain a mystery. She wrote few personal letters, kept no private journals, and had no confidant who knew her inmost thoughts. Two years before she died, she spoke to her parliament in words that show why, with all her faults and weaknesses, she was a great Queen: "To be a king and wear a crown is a thing more glorious to them that see it, than it is pleasant to them that bear it....It is my desire to live nor reign longer than my life and reign shall be for your good. And though you have had and may have many princes more mighty and wise sitting in this seat, yet you never had nor shall have any that will be more careful and loving."

The Queen went to her grave with medieval pomp as a new age began. The banners that ornamented her hearse were blazoned with devices that had meaning when kings in armor defended their crowns with the sword. But when Elizabeth was old and failing, and her former favorite, the Earl of Essex, attempted to seize her throne in order to found a dynasty, he was defeated by Robert Cecil, the bureaucrat, who crushed him by supporting the crown with a new kind of organised state power which made such a personal adventure meaningless. During the Queen's reign England had become a modern state, and the stage had been set for the next century's struggle between the Crown and Parliament for control of that organized power. The age of politics had begun.

43

CHRONOLOGY

1558: Elizabeth becomes Queen and makes William Cecil her secretary of state. **1559:** Mary Queen of Scots becomes Queen of France. **1560:** Civil war between Catholic and Protestant factions begins in France. **1561:** Driven out of France, Mary Queen of Scots returns to Scotland. **1563:** Protestant doctrine of the Church of England stated in the Thirty-nine Articles. **1564:** The king of Spain orders his viceroy to stamp out Protestantism in the Low Countries. **1565:** Mary Queen of Scots marries Darnley. **1566:** Darnley murders Rizzio. **1567:** Mary Queen of Scots marries Bothwell after Darnley is murdered, and is forced to abdicate. **1569:** A rebellion of Catholics in the north, led by the Earl of Northumberland, fails. **1570:** The Pope issues a bull of excommunication and deposition against Elizabeth. **1571:** Spain destroys the Turkish fleet in the battle of Lepanto. **1573:** The Dutch rebel against the Spanish. French Catholics massacre Protestants on St. Bartholomew's Eve. The Duke of Norfolk conspires with Mary Queen of Scots and is beheaded. **1576:** Burbage builds the first English theater. **1577:** Drake sets out on his voyage round the world in the Golden Hind. **1578:** The Dutch and English become allies. **1579:** Dutch Republic is proclaimed at Utrecht. Spanish troops land in Ireland. **1580:** Spanish occupy Portugal and claim all her overseas possessions. Jesuit agents spread subversion in England. **1581:** Golden Hind returns. Drake knighted by the Queen. **1582:** Spanish defeat combined French, English, and Portuguese fleet at Terceira. **1585:** English army lands in the Low Countries to join Dutch struggle against Spain. **1586:** Shakespeare comes to London. **1587:** Mary Queen of Scots beheaded. **1588:** Defeat of the Armada. **1589:** English army lands in France to aid Henri IV. **1590:** Marlowe's *Tamburlaine* and Sydney's *Arcadia* are published. Printing of Spenser's *Faerie Queen* begins. **1591:** English Azores squadron defeated by Spanish who regain command of mid-Atlantic. **1592:** Spanish again sweep English from mid-Atlantic. **1593:** Shakespeare's *Venus and Adonis* published. Henry IV crowned in Paris. Civil War in France ends. **1594:** Hugh O'Neill leads Irish rebellion. **1595:** France makes war on Spain. Drake's last raid on Spanish sea lanes fails. *Midsummer Night's Dream* performed. **1596:** John Donne is aboard a ship of the Anglo-Dutch fleet which raids Cadiz. **1597:** Anglo-Dutch army defeats Spanish at Turnhont. **1598:** William Cecil, Lord Burghley dies, his son Robert takes his place. The Globe Theatre built in Southwark. Ben Jonson's first comedies performed. **1599:** Essex sent into Ireland to put down Hugh O'Neill's revolt. **1600:** Essex returns to England and is beheaded for treason. **1601:** Spanish troops sent to Ireland to aid Hugh O'Neill, defeated at Kinsale and massacred. **1603:** Elizabeth dies and is succeeded by James I.

INDEX

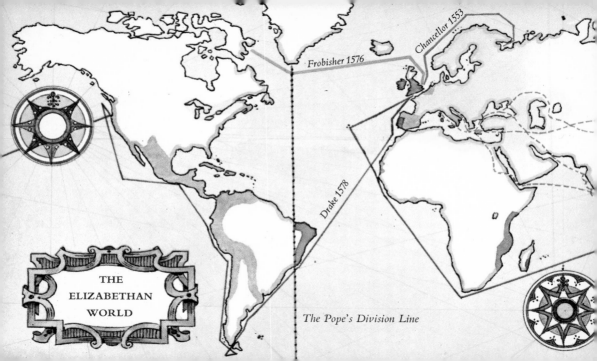

THE
ELIZABETHAN
WORLD

Frobisher 1576

Chancellor 1553

Drake 1578

The Pope's Division Line